TRIER: City and History

'Before Rome, Trier stood one thousand and three hundred years' – at least according to a medieval legend about the origins of the city. In fact, Trier's history begins in around the middle of the 1C BC, when Gaius Julius Caesar conquered Gaul and integrated the Moselle region into the Roman empire. In 16 BC Emperor Augustus recognised the strategic value of the location and established a city here: AUGUSTA TREVERORUM – City of the Emperor A... Treveri...

This makes Trier Germany's oldest city. It was the home of Roman emperors, and in later eras also of archbishops and princes elector, all of whom played a key role in the city's development. Many imposing historical buildings and monuments have survived to this day, bearing witness to Trier's former status as one of the great cosmopolitan cities of antiquity. The most famous landmark is the mighty Porta Nigra

Electoral Palais (Kurfürstliches Palais) ▽

('Black Gate'), the largest surviving Roman city gate north of the Alps. With its sheer size the single huge hall of the Roman 'Aula Palatina' (Constantine Basilica) still eloquently demonstrates the glory and power of the former Empire. The age of the prince bishops is also documented in many surviving buildings, including the cathedral (Dom) – Germany's oldest bishop church – and the Church of Our Lady (Liebfrauenkirche).

Towards the end of the 3C Emperor Diocletian made Trier – henceforth known as TREVERIS – his residence and the capital of the western territories of the Roman Empire. At the beginning of the 4C none lesser than Emperor Constantine himself resided here. Christianity spread further under his rule and more impressive buildings were constructed at his behest.

From 475 onwards Trier was held by the Franks. Following the Carolingian division of the empire the city was ceded to East Francia (later Germany) in 870 by the Treaty of Meersen. In the mid-10C the right to hold markets was granted for the Hauptmarkt square. In the age of the princes elector of Trier beginning in the 12C the city then experienced a chequered period of alternating blossoming and downfall.

After being held by the French since the end of the 18C the city passed to Prussia in 1815.

Today Trier is part of the German state of Rhineland-Palatinate (Rheinland-Pfalz). The Moselle metropolis has a population of over 100,000 and is the capital of its administrative district.

The countryside around Trier is particularly attractive. It is surrounded on all sides by the forests and mountain ranges of the Hunsrück and Eifel regions, and by the valleys of the Moselle, Saar and Ruwer rivers with their romantic vineyards. The Luxembourg border is just one minute's drive away, and neighbouring France and Belgium are also easily accessible. In addition to the imposing Roman monuments and world-famous excavations the city also boasts fascinating buildings dating from the Romanesque, Gothic, Renaissance and Baroque periods – all of them helping to bring Trier's rich history back to life.

There is no shortage of cultural attractions and entertainment in the university city. You can visit muse-

ums, art galleries and theatres, and a wide variety of interesting events are staged in the Europahalle.

Music is writ particularly large in Trier, with the many churches and historical buildings providing ideal venues for the many organ, chamber music and choral concerts. The courtyards of some of the buildings, such as the Simeonstift and the Electoral Palace, are also used for open air concerts.

Trier is the centre of the local wine-growing region, and you can try the outstanding wines of the Moselle, Saar and Ruwer in style in Germany's oldest wine cellars.

Many attractive cafés, restaurants and shops – especially those around the historical Hauptmarkt square – attract both locals and many visitors every day.

Hauptmarkt square and Simeonstrasse ▽

Circa 2050 BC
Legend has it that the city was founded '1,300 years before Rome' by Trebeta, stepson of Queen Semiramis.
Circa 53 BC
In the Gallic Wars (58-51 BC) the Romans under Gaius Julius Caesar conquer the territory of the rebellious Celtic Treveri.
Circa 16 BC
Emperor Augustus recognises the strategic advantages of the location and founds a city here: AUGUSTA TREVERORUM – City of the Emperor Augustus in the land of the Treveri.
1st Century AD
The city is promoted to the status of a 'Colonia', probably under the reign of Emperor Claudius (41-54 AD).
3rd Century
Trier is made capital of Gaul and together with Cologne becomes the residence of the Gallic Emperor Postumus (258-268).
Circa 275
The Franks and Germanic tribes drive deep into Roman territory and destroy the city. Shortly afterwards the Germans are then beaten back again by the Romans.
285
Under Emperor Diocletian Trier (now known as 'TREVERIS') becomes an imperial residence and the capital of the western territories of the Roman Empire.
4th Century
Constantine the Great resides in Trier from 306-316. In this period he rebuilds the city and creates impressive monuments.
Christianity spreads further under Constantine and Trier becomes an episcopal see. Trier's heyday lasts until nearly the end of the century.
Circa 400
Trier is abandoned as imperial residence and capital. The imperial court moves to Milan, the Prefecture to Arles in Southern France.
5th Century
Vandals, Suebs and Franks take Trier several times and destroy the city.
Circa 475/480
Trier falls to the Franks.
9th Century
After the Treaty of Verdun in 843 Trier remains part of Lothar's Middle Kingdom until 870, when it is ceded to East Francia (later Germany) by the Treaty of Meersen.
882
Invasion by the Normans and destruction of the city.
902
King Ludwig the Child grants sovereign rights to Archbishop Radbod.
958
The right to hold markets is granted for the Hauptmarkt square. Archbishop Heinrich has the market cross erected.
12th Century
Fortification of the city with a wall to the South. A second wall is built in 1134, closing the fortified ring around the city.
1143–1157
Establishment of a first citizen's association dedicated to obtaining political independence.
1192
The Archbishop of Trier is given the office of City Bailiff (Stadtvogt) and also becomes Supreme Judge.
1257
The Archbishops of Trier are made Princes Elector.
Circa 1302
The Trier Citizens' Council (Bürgerschaft) pushes through a new City Constitution. Now members of the citizens' guilds are also represented on the City Council, in addition to Schöffen (lay assessors) and Ministerialien (estate officials).
1307–1354
Reign of Archbishop Balduin of Luxembourg, brother of the German Emperor Heinrich VII and the great-

est of the princes elector of Trier.
He enlarges and forms the Electoral
State.
1473
The first university is opened and remains in operation until 1798, sponso-
red by the Trier Citizens' Council. The
imperial diet is held in Trier.
1512
Another imperial diet is held in Trier
under Emperor Maximilian. The holy
tunic of Christ is shown publicly in the
Cathedral Church (Domkirche) for the
first time.
1566–1580
The Citizens' Council fights in vain to
make the city 'reichsunmittelbar', i.e.
subordinate only to the emperor.
Emperor Rudolf II's ruling revokes
the city's independent status and
places it under the rule of an electoral
governor.
17th Century
In the Thirty Years' War Trier is ta-
ken first by the French and then by
imperial and Spanish troops, after
which the city once again becomes
French.
1674
During the campaigns of French Sun
King Louis XIV Trier is once again
embroiled in fighting with the French.
Many monasteries in and around the
city are destroyed by the troops of
General Vignory.
After 1714
A longer period of peace follows.
Economic conditions improve and the
city is rebuilt. Trier blossoms in fresh
glory.
1794/95
French revolutionary troops occupy
Trier, ushering in the end of the
Electoral State of Trier.
1798–1801
Closure of the university, dissolution
of the Electoral State. Trier is made
capital of the French department of
the Sarre.
1815
After the Congress of Vienna Trier
passes to Prussia and later becomes

the seat of the president of the administrative district.
1818
Birth of Karl Marx in Trier.
20th Century
World War I arrests economic
growth. Trier is occupied by the
French until 1930.
1944
Destruction of entire quarters of the
city in World War II.
1946
Trier becomes part of Rhineland-
Palatinate, one of federal Germany's
new Lander, or states.
1964
Completion of the canalisation
of the Moselle, opening of the
waterway between Koblenz and
Thionville.
1969
Incorporation of municipalities
makes Trier a major city with over
100,000 residents.
1970
Trier is once again a university city.
1984
Numerous celebrations mark the
city's 2,000th anniversary.
1987
Excavation of the third Roman
baths complex by the Cattle Market
(Viehmarkt).
1996
The holy tunic of Christ is displayed
publicly in Trier Cathedral for the
third time in the 20th century
(the last two times were in 1933 and
1959).
2004
Inauguration of the redesigned Kornmarkt (cornmarket).
2007
Exhibiton "Constantine the Great" in
three museums of Trier.
2008
First beatification in Trier Cathedral.
2010
Inauguration of the restored Balduin
Fountain.
2012
Holy Robe Exhibition.

Porta Nigra and Simeonstift

The Porta Nigra (Black Gate) – Trier's most famous landmark – is the biggest surviving city gate north of the Alps. Built in the last third of the 2C it is the northern gate of the city walls, which were originally 6.4 km long. The fortified building got its present name much later in the Middle Ages, when the light-coloured sandstone blocks turned grey-black with age. No mortar was used in the construction – the stone blocks were only held together with iron clamps cast into place with lead. The two semicircular towers projecting from the front of the Porta Nigra were originally the same height. A twin gate leads through the central structure, which encloses aninner courtyard open to the sky. The outer gates used to be secured with iron portcullises, and the inner openings could be blocked with wooden gates. The imposing monument is 36 m wide, and the west tower is around 30 m high. Following the conquest by the

▽ *Porta Nigra – City Museum Simeonstift*

△ *Porta Nigra*

Porta Nigra – Church of St Simeon in c. 1600 ▽

Franks at the end of the 5C the fortifications lost their original function. In the Middle Ages the city walls and all the other gates were torn down successively – only the Porta Nigra was preserved. In 1028 Simeon, a Greek hermit and friend of Archbishop Poppo of Trier, had himself wall-ed up in a small cell in the East Tower where he lived until his death in 1035. Afterwards Poppo established a Canons' Foundation (Simeonstift) in his honour and had the Porta converted into a twin church complex in the two upper storeys. The ground floor was filled in. A broad stairway led to the lay church on the first floor, and a separate outside stairway led to the collegiate church (Stiftskirche) above. In the first decades following 1800 the medieval addi- tions were removed from the original Roman gate, only leaving the choir apse. The buildings of the **Simeonstift** adjoin the Porta Nigra. It is Germany's oldest collegiate foundation and its structure is quite unusual: The clois-

◁ *Porta Nigra – interior*

Porta Nigra – Church of St Simeon in c. 1800 ▽

ter is not on the ground floor but on the first storey. Originally the cloister surrounded the beautiful inner courtyard on all four sides; today only parts have survived. The west wing was reconstructed in 1937–38. The Simeonstift complex houses the City Museum, the Tourist Information Bureau and a restaurant.

City Museum Simeonstift (Stadtmuseum)

The museum houses the art and cultural collections of the city of Trier. A large model shows what the city looked like in 1800. The Dormitorium (Gothic wooden ceiling) houses a sculpture collection, including the market cross of 958 and the original figures from the market fountain. The paintings collection includes a number of noteworthy works, and temporary exhibitions are also staged here.

▽ *City Museum Simeonstift*

▽ *City model „Trier in 1800"*

Cathedral (Dom)

Trier Cathedral and the Church of Our Lady (Liebfrauenkirche) originate from a double church built in the 4C. Two almost directly adjacent buildings, a south church and a north church, were constructed in 326 under Emperor Constantine on the site of the present cathedral and church. Legend has it they were built on the site of a former residential palace of Empress Helena (later St Helena). A baptistry (Baptisterium) stood between these two structures. The adjoining atriums and halls of the complex extended all the way to the present Hauptmarkt square. In around 380 the eastern section of the north church was altered and the Roman core was created – a quadratic structure with four huge granite columns (around 12 m high). In the period of the great migrations the Franks burned the old church building down to its outer walls. The columns collapsed and with them the flying buttresses and roof. A relic of one column of

Cathedral ▽

the square structure, the 'cathedral stone' (Domstein) can now be seen next to the doorway at the west apse. In the 6C Bishop Nicetius had the core structure of the cathedral rebuilt, using sandstone for the pillars. In the Passion Week of 882 the Normans stormed the city and destroyed the church once again. The next reconstruction was started by Archbishop Egbert (977–983), who had the old columns enclosed in a cross-shaped encasement. His powerful successor, Archbishop Poppo of Babenberg, continued the renovation work and the completed quadratic structure was consecrated in 1037. Poppo then began work on the extension of the cathedral and the west section, building the two towers and the west apse. Poppo died before the project was finished, however; the west section was completed by the two archbishops who succeeded him. In the 12C Archbishop Hillin added the Late Romanesque eastern choir with its polygonal apse and two towers to the church complex. The new altar was consecrated on May 1, 1196, and since then the Cathedral Consecration feast day (Domweihfest) has been celebrated on May 1 every year. The vaulting of the originally flat-roofed structure was added in the first decades of the 13C, together with the cloister connecting the cathedral and the Church of Our Lady. In around 1515 the southwest tower was made higher. The construction of the Heiltumskammer chapel for the holy tunic of Christ was planned in 1687 by Bishop Johann Hugo of Orsbeck. Work on the chapel, which was adjoined to the east choir, continued from 1702–1708. The transept by the master Baroque architect Judas was added during the renovation work following the fire of 1717. Several more renovation projects followed in the ensuing centuries, but no

Cathedral, high altar - organ ▷

more significant changes were made to the basic character of the cathedral. There is much worth seeing inside the building, including the stone statuary from the 12C and the Renaissance and Baroque periods (bishops' tombs, All Saints' Altar, front of the Heiltumskammer by J. W. Fröhlicher). The great Tympanum Portal leading from the cathedral to the Church of Our Lady dates from the 12C. The most important relic in the cathedral, the **holy tunic (Heiliger Rock),** is kept in the Heil-tumskammer. The original tunic of Christ for which the Roman soldiers diced is said to have been found in the 4C by the mother of the Roman Emperor Constantine, St Helena, who then had the garment brought from Jerusalem to Trier. The relic was kept hidden away from the public for many years, and in 1196 it was actually walled up in the new altar of the eastern choir. At the imperial diet held in Trier in 1512 the tunic was then exhibited in public for the first time at the order of

▽ *Holy Tunic Shrine (Heilig-Rock-Schrein) in the Heiltumskapelle*

Emperor Maximilian. Since then it has been shown sporadically at official pilgrimages, including those in 1933 and 1959. In 2012 pilgrims once again had the opportunity to see the holy tunic, which was put on display in a glass shrine in the centre of the cathedral from April 13 to May 13. The rich treasures of the cathedral (Domschatz) are exhibited in the so-called Badische Bau treasury by the cathedral cloister. Access to the treasury is through the side aisle. The exhibits include some of Germany's most important church treasures, mainly liturgical apparatus from former centuries. Other notable items: the Andreas portable altar (10C, an early masterpiece of the goldsmith's art), a late antique ivory plaque and a reliquary for the holy nail.

The "holy tunic" ▽

Church of Our Lady (Liebfrauenkirche)

The Church of Our Lady stands directly next to the cathedral. It is regarded as one of Germany's first Gothic churches, and its rotunda design gives it a unique status in the early Gothic period. The monumental structure is evidently modelled on churches in France, particularly the Cathedral of Reims. It was built from 1235–1260 on the site of the east section of the old south church. Four apsidial chapels form a Greek cross whose arms extend from the centre of the rotunda. Three of these are of exactly the same length, only the east choir is one yoke longer. Two smaller chapels are interposed between each pair of cross arms, giving the ground plan the form of a rose with twelve petals, the mystical symbol of Maria. The facade with the main doorway in the western arm is decorated with many carved figures. The vaulting over the crossing is around 35 m high, with twelve pillars (four thick

▽ *Cloister*

△ *West door*　　　　　　　　　　　　　　　　　　　　*Church of Our Lady* ▽

and eight slender ones) supporting the entire roof structure. These pillars are painted with depictions of the twelve apostles. A black stone in the floor marks the one point from where one can see all the apostles at the same time. Until 1631 the crossing tower was capped by a slender wooden spire around 80m high. After being destroyed by lightning the spire was replaced by a flat roof. The form of the windows is early Gothic; only the round arched windows of the crossing tower have Romanesque elements. The colourful glass windows of the choir are also noteworthy. Passing through the 'Paradise' – the northern vestibule connecting the cathedral and the Church of our Lady – one comes to the north door with a depiction of the coronation of Maria in its archway. There are also a number of interesting memorial stones in the 'Paradise'.

▽ *Church of Our Lady*

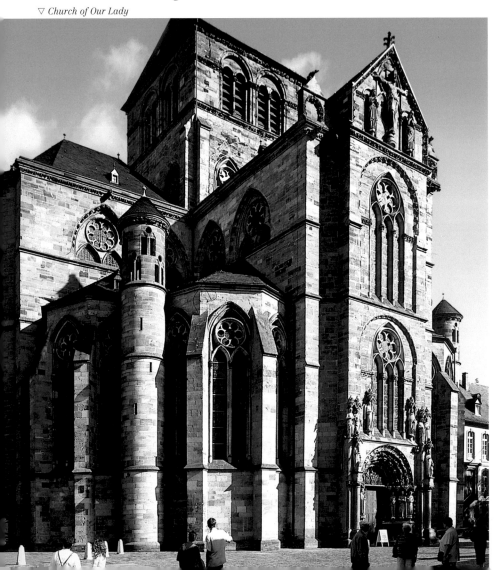

Museum at the Trier Cathedral

Since 1988 the museum has been housed in the former city prison (built by J. G. Wolff in 1830). The interior of the classicist building has been redesigned for its new purpose, but its exterior has been restored in its original form, with additions. The museum itself was founded in 1904 with collections drawn from archaeological excavations dating back to the mid-19C, when J. N. von Wilmowsky made extensive finds in the cathedral.

Since then exhibits from the entire bishop diozös see have been added to the collection. They include finds from early Christian cemeteries and the old double church complex. The magnificent Constantinian ceiling frescoes from the Imperial Palace found are particularly interesting. They were in 1945, and the around 50,000 fragments were recovered in two excavations and then reassembled in decades of painstaking work.

Picture of a woman, ceiling fresco from c. 320 ▽

Around the Hauptmarkt

The *Hauptmarkt (Main Market)* square forms the centre of Trier's Old Town. It is the venue for many events and folk festivals, and the regular markets are also still held here. The *St Peter Fountain (Petrusbrunnen)* in the south-east corner was built in 1595 by H. R. Hoffmann. Its central column is topped by a statue of the city's patron St Peter; the four figures below him depict the four cardinal virtues. The most striking building on the Hauptmarkt is the *Steipe,* built in 1430–83 as a festival and drinking house for the City Council. It gets its name from the supports of the open pointed arch arcades, which are called 'Steipen' in the local dialect. The four figures on the front of the ground floor depict the four city saints, the statues on the first floor two Knights of Roland. In 1944 both the Steipe and the *Red House (Rote Haus,* 1684) next door were destroyed, but they were then rebuilt. The inscription in golden letters

▽ *St Peter Fountain*

Red House ▽

▽ *Steipe*

Christmas market on Hauptmarkt square △

over the first storey windows of the Red House reads: 'ANTE ROMAM TREVERIS STETIT ANNIS MILLE TRECENTIS PERSTET ET AETERNA PACE FRUATUR. AMEN!' ('Before Rome Trier stood one thousand and three hundred years, may it continue to stand and enjoy eternal peace. Amen!'). Archbishop Heinrich I had the *Market Cross (Marktkreuz)* erected in 958 to commemorate the granting of the right to hold markets. The original cross is now in the City Museum; the present granite column is of Roman origin. *St Gangolf's* market church was probably founded in the 10C; it has been renovated several times with the addition of Baroque elements (14/15C) and a spire (beginning of the 16C). The interesting half-timbered patrician buildings around the square now house many restaurants, cafés and shops. The square provides an attractive venue for the annual *Christmas Market*.

◁ *St. Gangolf's*

Door of St Gangolf's ▽

△ *Half-timbered buildings*

Market Cross ▽

Kesselstadt Palace

K. M. Freiherr von Kesselstadt had the palace built in 1740–45. Rococo architect J. V. Thomann from Mainz succeeded in giving the frontage an elegant and attractive design, integrating it artfully into the difficult corner site.

House of the Three Kings (Dreikönigenhaus)

This late Romanesque/early Gothic patrician house with its palatial facade dates from the first half of the 13C. It is modelled on Romanesque residential towers. Originally there were no windows on the ground and first floors. The entrance was on the second floor and could only be reached by ladder.

Kornmarkt

The Neo-Baroque *Post Office* was built in 1881 (enlarged 1910), integrating architectural elements of the former Rococo Palace of 1759. The attractive Rococo *St George Fountain* (Georgsbrunnen) was designed by J. Seiz and built in 1750/51.

▽ *Kesselstadt Palace*

House of the Three Kings ▽

▽ *Post Office on the Kornmarkt square*

St George fountain ▽

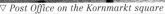

Thermal Museum on Viehmarkt

In Trier the ground is full of surprises. In 1987, work began on an underground car park at the Viehmarkt, but Trier's third and oldest thermal bath complex was discovered. This dates back to the early 2nd century. The car park was reduced and the thermal baths were protected. A glass cube was constructed above to plans by Cologne architect Oswald Mathias Ungers – a window into the city's history. Strong foundations, bathing pools, inflow pipes and waste water conduits, streets of houses and medieval buildings and the remains of a 17th century Capuchin cloister show the changing history of the location on the Roman Forum. In this way, we can experience history layer by layer and wall by wall. No wonder that people like to meet in this ambience, have a little refreshment or enjoy a stylish wine tasting.

▽ *Thermal Museum, interior*

▽ *Viehmarkt, St. Antonius*

▽ *Thermal Museum on Viehmarkt*

Roman Basilica • Aula Palatina

The Basilica is one of the most impressive buildings of late antiquity. Emperor Constantine the Great had it built in the early 4C on the remains of his former imperial palace. Originally the spacious residential complex included several large buildings; the Aula Palatina was probably the throne room or audience hall. It comprises a single huge rectangular building with an apse at the northern end. The ancillary buildings adjoined at the southern end, at right angles to the Basilica. The brickwork structure was originally plastered, and parts were painted in colour; remains of the paintwork can be seen around the edges of the windows. Two outside galleries made of wood originally stood below the rows of windows, providing a horizontal division in the structure. They were accessed via two spiral staircases to the right and left of the apse. The outside walls of the Basilica are 2.7 m thick. Inside, the hall measures 67 m long,

▽ *Emperor Constantine in Trier Cathedral*

▽ *Bronze coin of Constantinus II*

27 m wide and 30 m high - the imposing Porta Nigra would fit into the huge room twice over. Originally the interior of the hall was magnificently furnished, with costly marble panelling on the walls and golden mosaics in the niches. The entire black and white marble floor was heated from below (hypocaustum), and the walls were also heated. During the Frankish period the Basilica was used as a royal palace; from the 13C the 'Palatium' was the residence of the Archbishop of Trier. When the Electoral Palace was built in the 17C the Basilica was integrated into the new structure, removing large sections of the Basilica in the process. In the 19C, after a chequered history, the extensions were finally removed and the Basilica was rebuilt. In 1856 the building was turned into a Protestant church (Church of the Saviour). During World War II the building was completely gutted by fire. Postwar restoration, including the addition of a magnificent coffered ceiling, was completed in 1956.

Roman Basilica • Aula Palatina ▽ ▷▷

Electoral Palace – Petersburg Gate (Petersburg-Portal) and Red Tower (Roter Turm) △

Electoral Palace
Red Tower and Petersburg Gate

Construction of the buildings to the north and east of the later four-winged Petersburg Palace began in around 1615. Lothar von Metternich engaged the renowned architect Georg Riedinger for the project, and the palace was finally completed under Philipp von Sötern. The east and south walls of the Basilica were torn down to integrate it into the new complex. To the north of the Upper Palace a second courtyard was installed, around which the buildings of the Lower Palace were arranged. In 1756–61 the original south wing of the Electoral Schloss was replaced by the new Rococo Palace, and in the 19C the west wing was removed as part of the reconstruction of the Basilica. The Red Tower – which originally housed the Chancellery and Archive and is now the bell tower of the Basilica – and the Petersburg Gate of the Lower Palace have both been restored following damage during World War II.

◁◁ *Rococo staircase in the Electoral Palais (Kurfürstliches Palais)*

Electoral Palais

When Prince Elector J. Ph. von Walderdorff came to power in 1756 he was dissatisfied with the existing palace, and he made plans to redesign the entire complex. Only the south wing of the ambitious project – the Rococo Palace – was actually built, however. The prince had the plans drawn up by J. Seiz, a student of the brilliant architect B. Neumann. The sculptures are by F. Tietz. The garden frontage is now asymmetrical because part of the west wing was torn down during the rebuilding of the Basilica in 1944. A grand staircase bears witness to the magnificence of the original interior. The Rocaille balustrade by F. Tietz is regarded as a masterpiece of German Baroque. Tietz also produced the statues of the deities in the palace garden, which was reconstructed according to the original plans starting in 1981. Since the repair of the war damage in 1954–56 the palace has housed the offices of the regional administration.

Electoral Palais (Kurfürstliches Palais) ▽

St Barbara Baths (Barbarathermen)

In around 150 AD the Romans built the biggest baths of the antique world in the St Barbara quarter. The complex (various baths, indoor swimming pool, saunas, gym, changing and wash rooms etc.) remained in use for several hundred years. It was around 172 x 240 m in extent, and the interior and exterior of the buildings were clearly sumptuously fitted out. In addition to their practical function the baths were also an important social centre. After falling into disuse in later years the baths were then plundered for building material, and today only the foundations, cellar passages and remains of the impressive under-floor heating system (hypocaustum) have survived. Parts of the baths have been excavated and the finds testify to their former magnificence. They include an excellent Roman copy of the torso of an Amazon by the great Greek sculptor Phidias (State Museum).

▽ *St Barbara Baths*

Imperial Baths (Kaiserthermen)

Trier's 'youngest' historical baths were built under Emperor Constantine in the first half of the 4C, but they were never used for their intended purpose. When Constantine left Trier the spacious, symmetrical baths building was probably still an unfinished shell, and his successors remodelled it completely. Measuring 250 x 145 m, this complex too was one of the biggest baths of antiquity. In the Middle Ages it served as the corner bastion of the city walls, and a window of the caldarium was used as a city gate until the 19C. Several excavations have uncovered the entire complex, and following restoration and reconstruction work the original structure is now clearly visible. Interesting sights include several rooms, the fireplaces for the heating (praefurnias) and particularly the complex underground passage and piping systems, parts of which are on several levels.

Imperial Baths ▽

Amphitheatre

Dating from around 100 AD the oval arena is the oldest surviving Roman structure in Trier. One side of the stadium (approx. 70 x 50 m) was artfully integrated into the side of St Peter's Hill. Gladiatorial contests were presented here to audiences of up to 20,000 in three rows of stone seats. Originally the two halves of the oval were linked at the ends by three-arched gates with richly-decorated portals to the north and south. The two entrances to the audience area on the west side have survived. The original imperial box was located between them. The chambers open to the arena behind the perimeter wall were probably animal cages. It is still possible to visit the cellars, and the original Roman rainwater drains are still functional. In the 2C the amphitheatre was integrated in the city fortifications and in the 19C it was used as a quarry for building material.

▽ *Amphitheatre*

Karl Marx House

The philosopher and economic and social critic was born in this typical plain Trier family house in 1818. Shortly after his birth his family moved to the Simeonstrasse. Today the Karl Marx House contains a museum operated by the Friedrich Ebert Foundation, with extensive documents on the life and work of Marx.

IN DIESEM HAUSE
WURDE AM 5.MAI 1818
KARL MARX GEBOREN

Karl Marx House △ ▽

Guilds Fountain
(Handwerkerbrunnen)

Designed in the form of an oak tree by K. Apel the brass fountain includes signs and figures depicting the 42 craftsmen's guilds of the district.

University

Trier University is now located on the Tarforster Plain high above the city. The modern, futuristic buildings make an interesting architectural contrast to the historical structures of the Old Town. Trier's first university was founded in 1473. It was closed by the French in 1798 and then finally reopened in 1970. It now has five faculties: Economics, Law and three humanities departments. Since 1952 the university also has a cooperation agreement with the Trier Theological College.

△ *Guilds Fountain*

△ *Central station*   *University* ▽

State Museum
(Rheinisches Landesmuseum)

The 'Rhinish Provincial Museum of Trier' was originally founded in 1877, and it received its first home in 1889. Its original exhibits included the collections of the 'Society for Useful Research' and the mineral collections of the city. In the course of time rich archaeological finds made several extensions necessary – the last was completed in 1987. It is now one of Germany's most important archaeological museums, with 7,000 m² of exhibition rooms with four departments – Prehistory, Gallo-Roman, Merovingian/Frankish and Medieval/Modern. Interestingly, all the exhibits on show are from Trier and the surrounding area. The *Prehistory Department* includes finds from the Stone, Bronze and Iron Ages (weapons, tools, jewellery and vessels). The 'Hunsrück-Eifel Culture' is treated as a special local group, and there is also a separate section devoted to handicrafts in the Latène style.

State Museum ▽

Mosaic in the State Museum ▽

The *Gallo-Roman Department* is particularly extensive, with a number of impressive floor mosaics, including the magnificent charioteer mosaic from the Imperial Baths. Many masterly sculptures are also on show, such as the torso of an Amazon from the St Barbara Baths (copy of an original by Phidias). The famous Neumagen Tombstones are also noteworthy, including stone fragments showing the 'Happy Helmsman' and the 'Neumagen Wine Ship'. These and other tombstones showing scenes from mythology and daily life of the time can be seen in the museum's 'Tombstone Row'. The largest surviving example of these tombstones is the Igel Column, the original of which now stands in Igel, a village near Trier. An extensive collection of Roman glasswork includes the famous and interesting 'Diatrete glass'. The *Merovingian/Frankish Department* includes a particularly interesting ivory relief showing Abraham with his seven faithful

▽ *Mosaic of the victorious charioteer Polydus/Trier c. 250 AD*

followers. Noteworthy exhibits in the *Medieval/Modern Department* include a Romanesque capital with the four rivers of Paradise and a cast-iron relief showing the Virgin Mary and Child.

▽ *Diatrete glass, 4C*

▽ *Neumagen wine ship*   *Igel column (original)* ▷

St Paulinus' Church (St. Paulin)

The original Romanesque church on this site was built to house the bones of St Paulinus. It and its successors were all destroyed – the last in 1674 by General Vignory. Work on the present church of St Paulinus began under Archbishop F. G. von Schönborn in 1734, and the completed building was consecrated in 1757 under J. Ph. Walderdorff. The initial plans were drawn up by Ch. Kretschmar, and the work was then completed by the famous architect B. Neumann. The plainness of the nave's exterior is only broken by the spire at the end. This makes the contrast of the magnificent, jubilant Rococo glory of the interior of the former collegiate church all the more overwhelming. A series of major artists have contributed to the wonderfully sumptuous decorations of St Paulinus, including Arnold, Scheffler, Seiz and Tietz. Particularly interesting: stucco work, sculptures, ceiling frescoes and the magnificent high altar.

▽ *St Paulinus' Church*   *St Paulinus', interior with high altar* ▷

Zurlauben

This area on the Zurlauben Riverbank used to be the site of a fishermen's and sailors' village. The lovely houses are nearly 200 years old. On the other side are gardens with pavilions and summerhouses covered with ivy and vines. Today the visitor can while away pleasant hours in the traditional pubs and restaurants. This is where you start for lovely excursions on the idyllic river Moselle.

Old Moselle River Cranes

Up to the 18C the Moselle was a busy trade route and cranes were needed to load and unload the ships. The Old Crane was built in 1413, the Customs Crane further upriver went into service in 1774. Both cranes have the same construction, with a rotating conical roof and two jibs. Rollers on the jibs guided the hoisting cables into the winches inside, which were powered by pedal wheels. The mechanisms are still intact.

▽ *Zurlauben*

▽ *Old Moselle river crane*

Virgin Mary Column
(Mariensäule)

Standing on a steep slope the Virgin Mary Column rises up 300 m above sea level. The 40 m tower is topped by a statue of the Virgin Mary. Inaugurated in 1866, the monument was financed by donations from the citizens of Trier to commemorate the proclamation of the dogma of the immaculate conception of Mary. In the evening the monument is attractively illuminated.

Roman Bridge
(Römerbrücke)

Five of the surviving seven piers date back to Roman times. The bridge was built in the 2C; it is the third structure in almost exactly the same place. The original piers have a cast mortar core and a cladding of basalt blocks held together by iron clamps. Until the Middle Ages the superstructure was made of wood. The present bridge arches were built in 1717/18.

△ *Virgin Mary Column (Mariensäule) with view of Trier*　　　　*Roman Bridge (Römerbrücke)* ▽

Tourist information Trier, town and region

Discover Germany´s oldest town! The tourist information helps you with a wide range of competent and friendly service. This is the place to go to for information and tips! They offer many guided tours and adventure tours for single travellers and for groups. The team will be glad to help you exploring the impressive buildings and cultural monuments as well as the whole region around the rivers Moselle, Saar, Sauer and Ruwer. The tourist information is located in the city centre next to the Porta Nigra. The integrated Trier shop offers you a large range of products, literature about Trier and surroundings, maps for hikers and cyclists, gifts, Trier fashion, wines and a lot more. With the attractive "Trier-Card" you can use all the city busses and you´ll get many reductions during your stay in Trier.

INFORMATION • ADDRESSES • OPENING HOURS

TRIER DIALLING CODE

+49-(0)651

INFORMATION

Trier Tourismus und Marketing GmbH
Simeonstraße 60, D-54290 Trier
☏ 97808-0, Fax 97808-76
info@trier-info.de
www.trier.de
January–February:
mo–sa 10–17h, su 10–13h
March–April:
mo–sa 9–18h, su 10–15h
May–October:
mo–sa 9–18h, su 10–17h
November–December:
mo–sa 9–18h, su 10–15h
24 and 31 December: 10–13h

CITY TOURS

City Walking Tour
Big and short bus tour
City walking tour (2h)
Toga tour
Tour with the ministrel singer
Tour for Night Owls
Walking Tour for children
CitySightseeing Hop On - Hop off:
April–October daily 10–17h
25 November – 22 December 10–17h
Römer-Express
April–October: daily 10–18h, every 25 min.
Nov., Dec. + March: daily 10–17h hour clock
Sa–Su every half-hour
January–February: sa/su 10–17h hour clock
in suitable conditions.
Tickets available from the driver or at the
Tourist-Information. ☏ 97808-0

SIGHTS

**Porta Nigra, Imperial Baths, Amphitheatre and
St Barbara Baths**
October+March: daily 9–17h
April–September: daily 9–18h
November–February: daily 9–16h
Thermal Museum on Viehmarkt
☏ 9941057, www.trier-info.de
January–December: 9–17h
First business day of the week closed.
Last admission 30 min. before closing.
Roman Basilica – Aula Palatina
☏ 994912 0-0, Fax 994912 0-20
trier@ekkt.de
www.konstantin-basilika.de
Cathedral-Information
☏ 979079-0
info@dominformation.de
www.dominformation.de

Cathedral
April–October: daily 6:30–18h
November–March: daily 6:30–17:30h
Cathedral Treasury
January–March: tu–sa 11–16h
Sundays and public holidays 12:30–16h
April–December: mo–sa 10–17h
Sundays and public holidays 12:30–17h
Church of Our Lady
April–October 8–19h (su – 18h)
November–March 8–17h
St Matthew's Abbey Church
☏ 32634, daily 8–19h
except on sunday mornings
St Paulinus' Church
☏ 270850
mo, we–sa 9–17h
tu 11–17h, su 10–19:30h

MUSEUMS

City Museum Simeonstift (Stadtmuseum)
(at the Porta Nigra), ☏ 718-1459/54
tu–su 10–17h
State Museum (Rheinisches Landesmuseum)
Weimarer Allee 1, ☏ 9774-0
landesmuseum-trier@gdke.rlp.de
www.landesmuseum-trier.de
tu–su 10–17h
Museum at the cathedral
Bischof-Stein-Platz 1, ☏ 7105255
museum@bistum-trier.de
www.bistum-trier.de
tu–sa 9–17h
Sundays and public holidays 13–17h
Karl Marx House, Museum
Brückenstrasse 10
☏ 97068-0, Fax 97068-140
info.trier@fes.de, www.fes.de/marx/
November–March: mo 14–17h, tu–su 11–17h
April–October: daily 10–18h
Toy Museum
Dietrichstraße 51
☏ 758 50, Fax 994 38 75
info@spielzeugmuseum-trier.de
www.spielzeugmuseum-trier.de
January–March: tu–su 11–17h
April–December: tu–su 11–18h

MOSELLE CRUISE SHIPS

Personenschiffahrt Gebr. Kolb oHG
Trier Agency, Georg-Schmitt-Platz 2
☏ 26666, Fax 26337
Event- and Charter Tours
Day trips and Excursions
Departures: Zurlaubener Ufer,
(near Porta Nigra)
Tickets and reservations:
Tourist Information Trier, ☏ 97808-0 or
www.moselrundfahrten.de

St Matthew's
(St Matthias)

The Benedictine abbey and parish church of St Matthew lies in the south of the city. The predecessor of the present church was built in an early Christian Roman cemetery outside the city fortifications. Trier's first bishops (St Eucharius and St Valerius) were buried in crypts here in the 4C and 5C. The 3C Albana crypt has survived and is open to the public. The present Romanesque church was built in 1127–60. When the old church of St Eucharius was pulled down to build it the grave of the Apostle Matthew was found – it is the only apostolic grave north of the Alps and still a popular place of pilgrimage. The name was then changed from St Eucharius to St Matthias. The late Gothic net vaulting was built in around 1500, the early classicist balustrades of the towers were added in the 18C.

▽ *St Matthew's*